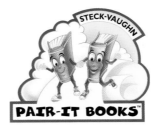

STECK-VAUGHN

PAIR-IT BOOKS™

Changing Colors

Written by Gare Thompson

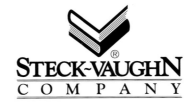

STECK-VAUGHN
COMPANY

A Division of Harcourt Brace & Company

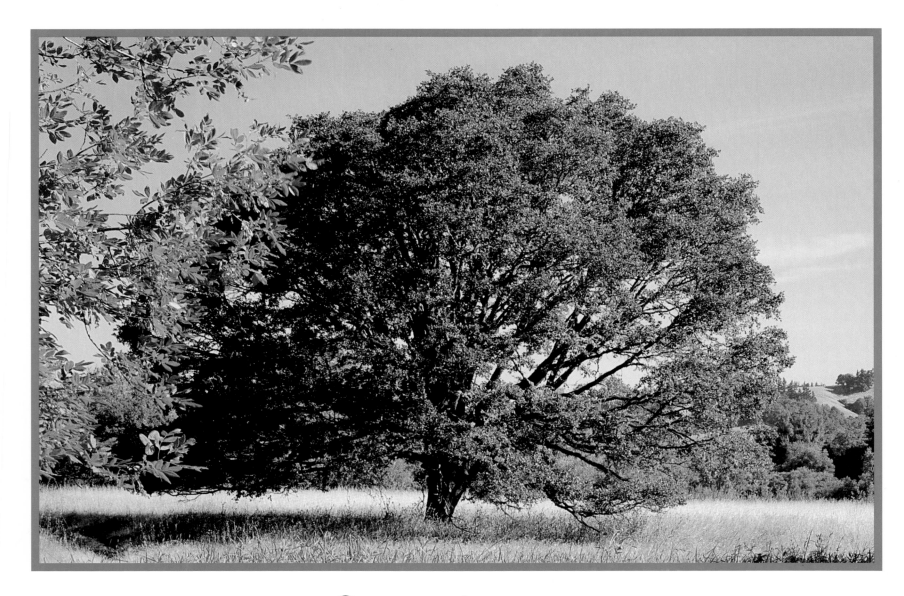

Green leaves

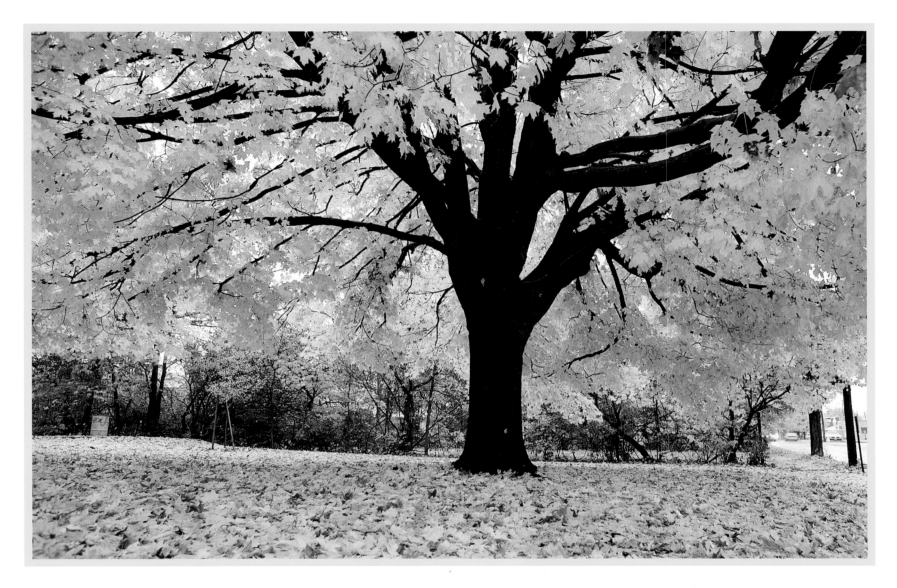

Yellow leaves

3

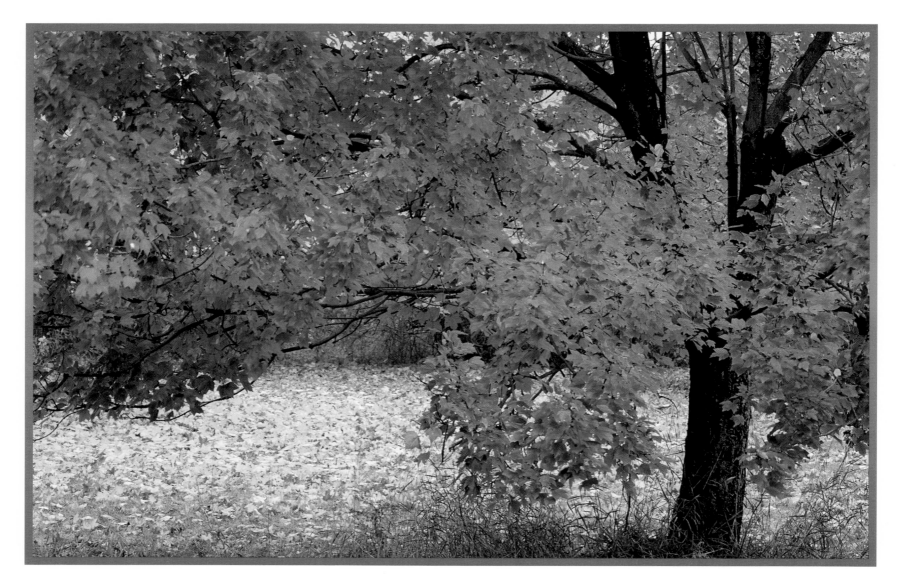

Red leaves

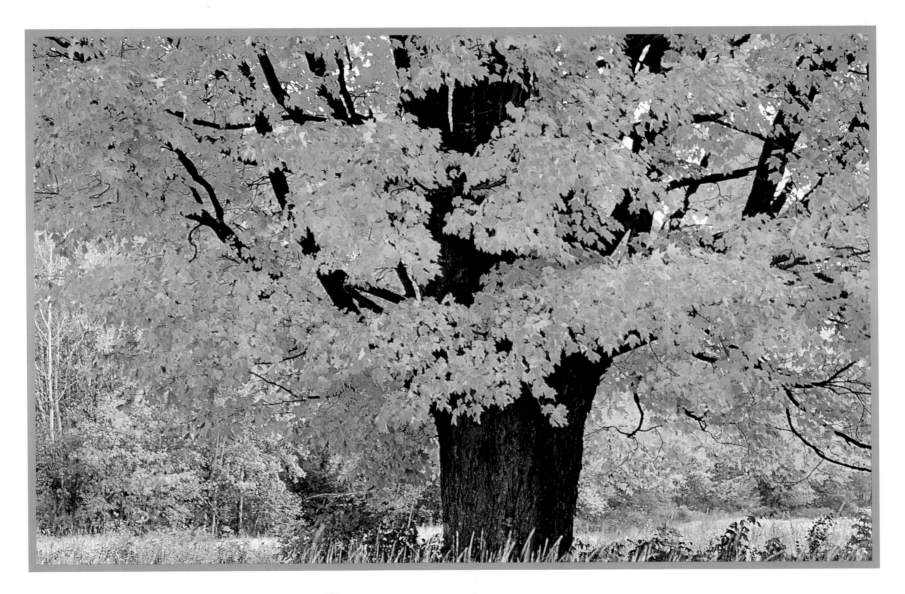

Orange leaves

5

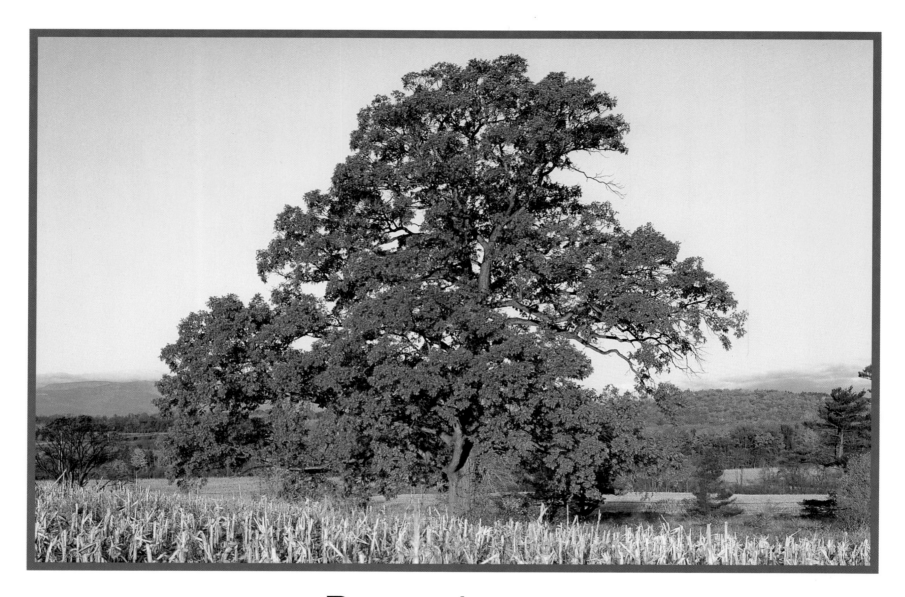

Brown leaves

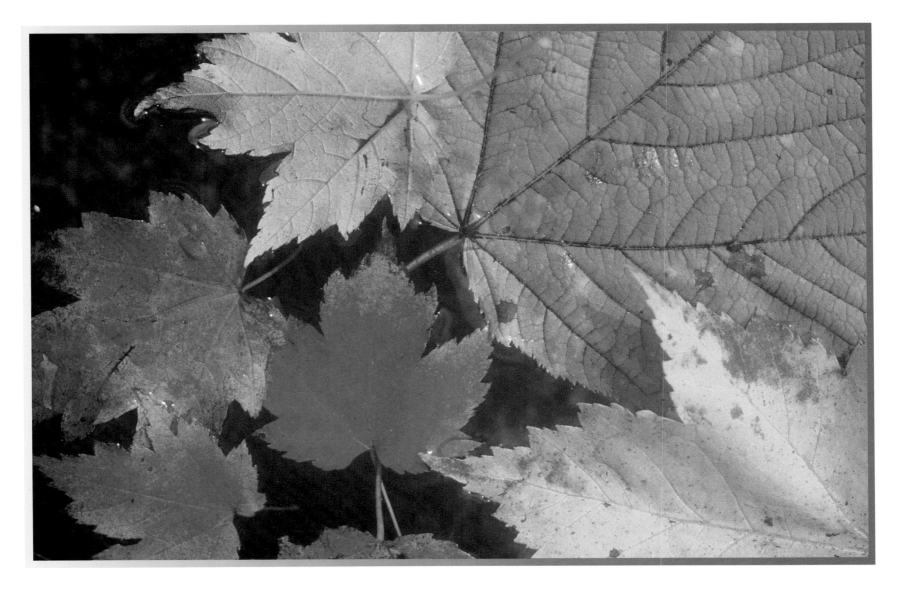

Many colors

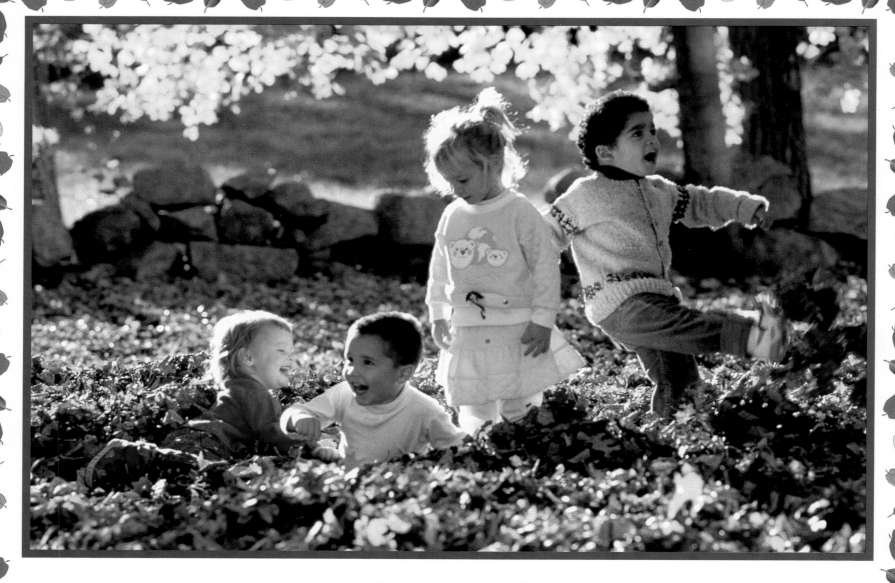

Jump in!